Sunflower

SERA HOLLAND

Sunflower

Dedicated to me.
I deserve it. All of it.

"my true vocation –
keeping an eye on things
whether they existed or not"
—Billy Collins

Table of Contents

Oops

Oh dear,
seems I've mistaken
the churning waves
for butterflies.

Happy Birthday

There's a photo on my desk of me, age five
chin turned up, like a sunflower.

My hair is cut short, bangs hang on my forehead.
I want to be an astronaut when I grow up.
My favorite flowers are sunflowers.

Nobody tells sunflowers how to smile,
how to wear their petals.
They can stare at the sun all day long.
When I try, I hurt my eyes.

I planted sunflower seeds
in the front garden by the blue bench. Everyday,
I check for inflorescence.

They never grew. I never watered them.
Nobody else even knew they were there.

Inflorescence

In second grade, I wrote a haiku.
  World's toughest rodeo,
  bull-riding, broncos, cowboys.
  Monkey on a dog?
    The syllables were off but,
    that was all it took.
    I was in love. Obsessed. I learned cursive
    on the stage in the auditorium,
    auditioned for a never-ending life of half-
    loops scribbled across napkins,
    the back of old tests,
    the margins of my favorite books.
    I would've written on the walls if I could.
      On my birthday, I wished for a pen
      that would never run out,
      a journal no one else could read.
        Pencils could never keep up.
        I haven't put one down,
        since.

My Brother's Teeth

My brother's tooth turned black and had to be pulled
because he hit his face on the dashboard
when my mom hit the brakes on purpose.

He's never had a cavity,
but I hid inside mine.
A sweet tooth to bore the holes deeper,
to make sure my growing body would fit.
I sleep inside them now.

I'm trying to unlearn my nostalgia
for a time when I was afraid to open my mouth.
My teeth might turn black. What if
the other kids laughed. They'd know
I hadn't brushed like I was supposed to.

I can't miss the time I was told to smile right,
decided maybe I didn't want to smile at all.

Atacama

Across the world, a desert
five hundred years without rain.
I wish I could build a sandcastle,

sleep amongst the lizards,
drink from the cacti.
Here, more temperate.

The clouds always part – I know this.
The rain always stops – I know this.
The wind always hushes.

When the sun is hiding, I miss her.
I wonder if she misses me, too.

A Lot Like Growing Up

The first time it floods, novelty.
You marvel open-mouthed at how quickly the street fills,
and you wade through it, waist-deep,
not caring that is smells of sewage,
not noticing what's bobbing near the surface.

The second time it floods,
the waterline rises higher than your anticipation,
laps at the baseboards and the bottom step.
Sulfuric sweet penetrates the walls,
lingers on the ground floor for weeks.

The third, fourth, fifth time it floods,
your anxiety ebbs, barricaded by sandbags.
Disappointment, bitter self-betrayal.

The eighth time it floods,
you remember the first time
the gutters couldn't handle the swell,
spewed like college girls on St. Patrick's Day.

The fifteenth, twentieth time it floods,
just Tuesday.

Colorado

I thought it would be better because the trees were taller,
evergreen. I thought the mountains would welcome
me home. I thought I'd wake up to the sun shining brighter.
I thought the thinned air would make my lungs stronger.

The grass only grew from June to July,
the trees wore white shrouds, towered above me.
My voice echoed through their stems, through crevasses,
echoed back to remind me
not even oxygen wanted my company.

How to Make a Cup of Coffee

STEP ONE: Get the fuck out of bed.
Smooth out the creases
of your outline in the dirty sheets.

STEP TWO: Shake off the dust,
wring out your bones.

STEP THREE: Welcome the hardwood beneath your
clammy feet, the crackling in your knees,
remember how to move your muscles
again.

STEP FOUR: Fill the water and grounds.
Forget what realm you're in.
Feel your shoulders weighing down,
hands like dumbbells.
Gravity is a greedy, bloodthirsty bitch
and your posture fucking sucks.

STEP FIVE: Pour the coffee in a mug.

STEP SIX: For a minute, the aroma will bring you back
to reality. For a minute,
you'll feel kind of okay.

STEP SEVEN: Take a sip and burn your tongue.
Whatever.

STEP EIGHT: Get back in bed.
                               Skip work.
                               Don't shower. Repeat.

Sometimes it just doesn't have a happy ending.

Parking Garage

No one knows which fell faster: her body,
or the sinking in her heart
as she watched the yellow line grow nearer,
until it turned black.

Nobody knows if she feels better,
but the impact of her knees buckling against her skull
cracked across the city
or, at least,
it keeps replaying behind my eyes.

Now, the teachers speak in whispers,
as the students fill the parking lot with daisies, tea candles,
Valentine's Day teddy bears.

The firemen will wash her away,
a splattered dragonfly on the windshield.
Cars will roll over the rose-petal stain on the concrete,
none the wiser.
In three days, they'll forget about it.

Corpse flower

Congratulations,
you graduated from the playground,
peeling the pink from your lips in the snow,
until blue, raw steak, bloody fingernails,
someone said you're too loud,
your friends laughed.

Congratulations,
you won the fist fight
against the brick wall around the corner
where no one could watch you, hoped
a knuckle would snap, glad it didn't,
saw it in a movie once.

Congratulations,
no one wanted to listen to you
explain your love affair with safety pins,
just scratching the surface,
too afraid to go deeper,
coward.

Congratulations,
at twenty-four you bury seeds
of frustration, topsoil fists,
purple and green blossoms on your thighs,
immediate resentment,
lie about it later.

Congratulations,
you convinced everyone
you're just *so* clumsy,
fell in a rosebush, fell in the hallway,
tripped on a run, blame the concrete,
tree branches hanging too low.

Congratulations,
on becoming a woman,
on still fighting walls, still throwing mirrors,
throwing punches where kisses should be,
throwing your forehead into hardcover books,
bathing your fingers in blood from your lips,
savoring the burn, the salt,
childish.

Mason

I told you I didn't want to learn how to shoot a gun.

I didn't want you to wrap your arms around me,

square my hips from behind like they do in movies,

because I didn't want you to blame yourself when the bullet
lodged between the aluminum walls of my sinuses

was engraved with your name,

because every time I imagined my hands

wrapped around the grip,

I envisioned the barrel turned around,

the ringing in my ears,

the muffled pop across the river.

Buried

When my time comes,
let nothing separate my rotting flesh from soil.

Take what's needed, bury the rest,
and let me be forgotten.

Lightning Strike

The reverb between the riverbanks chased away the blackbirds. Further, where the wind erased the rapids, the old man startled awake. Blinking, slowly, he stood – a bit startled at this rude awakening. He stretched his arms towards the cotton clouds, fingertips brushing their edges. To his left, a murmur through the grass. To his right, a honeybee. He felt the pinprick panic of the ants on his feet well before he felt the searing in his temple, before he noticed the smoke trickling from his nostrils, before the coughing. *I've never been much of a smoker*, he joked, and counted his fingers and toes.

When he felt the first raindrop, he shrugged, and drifted back to sleep.

Lightning from
the Perspective of Ants

How quickly the swarm unfolded, a force majeure, without the precursory flash. The strike too precise, as if God couldn't contain himself, extended His forearm, His index finger, to unfurl the cardstock leaves and run His palms over the velvet, but withdrew upon that first touch. From below, a nearby ant saw the soot as it billowed from the trunk, rushed away and back, away and back, as did they all, away and back, each carrying a single water droplet, panicked well wishes. For once, caring about something other than themselves. Each worried thought surprising benevolence, each prayer a selfless wish for grace.

Absence

On his deathbed, aware of his mortality,
he was ready.

I don't know if I'll ever be.

Mount Celestial

The white paneled church
with the boarded-up windows
a time capsule from 1998.

Next door, a half marked grave caving in.
Six feet underneath,
the casket inching down the hillside.

I wonder where her other half is buried.
Perhaps, alongside his newer soulmate?

Or perhaps, he expired alone,
with no one to care where the body
was drained and dumped.

I wonder what felt better:
the betrayal,
or her death.

Mourning

It hung humid in the room
squeezed itself between sweaters and skin
     hypothermic
rang violently
in the silence between laughs.

In the pause before smiles flipped,
it bubbled in the back of throats.
grabbed with clenched fists,
pulled our stomachs down.

The sinking
     in our chests
         repeated,
broken records,
the same jokes, reminiscent,
the same guilty grief
    this is all my fault,
    if only I had told him to suck it up,
    go home.

Soul-searching

I went to your ghost and asked how to find your body.
They said "look under the roundest stones
on the grassiest hillsides, look from the highest treetops
and under the smallest mushroom caps".

I went to your body and asked how to find your mind.
They said, "walk through the fields of lavender,
past the sunflower plantations, wade through the creek
and say 'hi' to the salmon".

I went to your mind and asked how to find your soul.
They said, "silly girl, silly girl, there is no soul".

Nurture

I.   The old quilt you drape over your legs while
you watch television,

    silence from the street drifting through

    the window makes the furniture sticky,

    mid-morning stillness, jaunty.

    You're eight years old and you're sick and you're eating
peaches straight from the can

    in the living room, and you're quite excited

(even though your stomach bristles)
(even though you must nap with a towel
beneath your head)

because you never get to eat in the living room.
Mom brings you ginger ale.
You watch *Jeopardy*, *Wheel of Fortune*,
PBS Kids until it's time for dinner.

II. You're older and sickness is less like a skipped
 stone ripple in the pond down the road,
 more like a rip tide. You fake sick
 to get out of school just like the bad kids did,
 not out of fear —
 math tests, changing in the locker room —
 but a desperate craving for that booming quiet,
 the pounding calm you keep inviting in but
 never comes. You think
 I can crush my ribs with peace,
 a weighted blanket.
 I'll feel better if
 I fold open my ears.
 It will funnel until I'm up to my eyes in
 tranquility.

 You can't keep dinner down. You try,
 end up going to bed feeling worse than waking.

Codes & Keys

The further I get from fourteen,
the better the soundtrack sounds.
I mean, how many times did I listen to this album?
How many times did I lose my voice from singing?
How many nights did I lie awake, too tired to sleep, with
the CD playing? Fourteen was the year I started running.
In converse, no less. I didn't stop
until the shin splints gave me a limp.
It's been ten years and I still can't run two miles.
I still listen to the same album.
It still reminds me of the year the love bugs swarmed
against the windows,
the year the streets became a swimming pool,
and we swam and swam
until the storm was over.
The memory of brown water on my lips
tastes better than twenty-four,
because now I care about tetanus, now I'm manic,
and I still can't fucking sleep.
The further I get from fourteen, the more I forget
I'm aging. The more I forget what I'm running from.

Autumn

After class, I'm rushing through the piles on the curb.
Amidst the amber rain, inhaling mouthfuls of musk,
getting high on the terpene, chasing it with cocoa.

I believe in magic because it's twinkling
like Christmas lights. I'm covering it in maple syrup
and chewing, feeling the pinprick in my nostrils,
pulling my scarf a little higher,
before Mom calls me inside.
It's getting too dark.

In the morning, the trickle in the gutter,
mud puddles in the grass,
my cheek pressing against the glass,
fogging up the window,
wondering if it really happened.

Afterlife

If he didn't go to heaven, where did he go?
Is he floating through the air,
just popping by to say "hello!"
from inside the raindrops?
Is he flowing through the copper,
flickering the lights?
Is he crackling the bacon grease,
the morning after his wake?
Was he assuring me he was fine
when I was burned by hot oil?

Daylight Savings

I.   Eventually, you find yourself drawing the
            evening closed earlier, just like the curtains,
            get lost in your dreams quicker, easier,
            the outskirts of Neverland
            the belly of the whale,
            it's not even seven P.M.
            Set the clocks back, tedious.
            One always overlooked,
            lingering an hour behind.

II.   December and January forget what the yard looks like,
            the wind whistles
            hollow through the branches,
            eerie through the doorframe.
            The trees can't hold it back anymore.

III.   The self-help books say
            winter must be endured
            for spring to be welcomed.
            You think they're full of shit.

IV.   Sure enough, round the corner,
            magnolia buds come calling.
            Here come the birds, the daffodils,
            watch your shadow grow shorter,
            watch your step on the muddy sidewalk.
            Sighing as the clocks turn forward,
            just as tedious, almost haunting.

Daisy Chain

Sprouting from my eyelashes, underneath my fingernails.
They climb over my windows,
clouding my view of the sun.
They reach through cracks in the foundation,
grasping for the inside air.

They grip my ankles, then my calves,
until my body is a garden,
and they lower me back to bed.
When I close my eyes,
I dream of their yolks.

Sometimes, I want to be the dusty pollen.
To be gathered in little satchels and taken far, far away.

Sometimes, I want to be the stems after the last frost.

Until then, I'll carry them in bouquets
keep them in vases on the kitchen table,
keep them as an option.

Columbia

Take my hand and lead me back
to the crumbling white house
with the creaky front porch steps,
musty, cigarette smoke.

Lead me through the crowded basement
with the rock band, the dirt floor.
Ruin my shoes again and sing to me
loud words I can't understand.

Take my hand and lead me back to the night
I left my worries in the glow of suburban streetlights.

Laguna

Drinking vodka from coke bottles, new moon.
Hanging our laced shoes from the lifeguard stand.
Dark water beyond beached kelp, drunk.
Socks dripping, my pants soaked with salt and sand.

Our faceless shadows laugh, voices carry west
across the pacific. Good memories
recounted between lost friends. Planning futures,
reunions beneath the palm trees.

When the sun is gone, our vision blurs.
The world's edge feels more beautiful.
Platonic love distracting, here I am
forgetting to plan my own funeral.

Self-forgiveness becomes an afterthought.
Breathe in. Out. Throw up in the parking lot.

Remember it forever.

Polycarpic

Some flowers bloom only once
before their petals senesce.

How lucky we are
to bloom again and again.

Go Home

Spanish moss curtains
drape over the old oak trees.
Bald cypress knees peek out from the silt
by the bayou. Palmettos frolic beneath the canopy
as cicadas sing of darker days
when the flood threatened to whisk them away.

This is where I come to preen my feathers,
to pull the ticks from my flesh,
where the coyotes' playful yelps lull me to sleep.

This is where I fledged.
Maybe this is where I'll expire.
Maybe this is my home after all,
nestled in the bend of the Brazos.

My Love

She's curled up on the corner of my mattress, fast asleep
and warm. She's around the hallway corner in the
morning, begging. I never mind.
She knows when I wake up.
We never miss a morning together.
She knows when I get home.
There she is, right behind the door, big-tooth grin,
screaming *where have you been all day?*
and *I missed you, don't you know?* I wonder if she knows
she's my best friend. I wonder if I'm hers too.
I wonder if she knows she saved my life.
All those late nights wanting,
knowing if I stepped out, she'd be devastated,
knowing I'd miss her too much.
Sometimes, I can't find her, and I search high and low,
only to discover her sunbathing by the glass door, supine.
Sometimes, she crawls into my lap, and I never mind
when she kneads my legs, chomps the corners
of my hands because she's purring
so loud. It makes me wonder how I ever hated cats.
When I was little, I got clawed in the cheek by a stray.
Maybe it was a premonition.

Nature

Your skin is softer than the hand-stitched afghan,
twice as resilient, thrice as comforting.
The gilt in your irises washes me
in an amber glow. Golden coins on the ocean floor.
I'm floating in the waves.

Slipping into bed with you is jumping in the pool.
Here, it's always summer vacation, afternoons,
cannonballs, no more permission slips,
no more visits to the nurse.
Sometimes, no more speaking at all. But, if we must,
the whispers cascading from your tongue
taste like peaches.
Smack your lips together, a hint of ginger.

That serene I've been fiercely searching for
flows from you like a spring, and I feel full,
and I feel tired, post-thunder relief,
jovial, laugh in my belly
knowing when I dry again, you'll be the rain,
knowing I can dance in it.

Sunflower

I'd like to believe things will go my way.
Stars will align in my favor, for once,
I'd like to think

for once, I deserve it.
Not selfish, for once. The four-leaf clovers
I've hoarded finally pay off.

I've saved at least twenty-four.
At most, a normal human life span.
What's that, seventy?
Seems doable,

for once, if the cards are drawn right.
Seems like it could be golden after all.
Seems like the sun shines

bright behind the clouds, seems like
it will keep rising. For once,
it seems like the flowers are smiling back.

My Therapist Calls
This Being Present

I can feel the very tips of my fingers
the ridges where they leave their prints,
my feet, their peeling heels,
the highest peak of my nose, my chin,
my bottom lip scabbing over.
Finally, inhabiting every corner of my body
again
though I'm not sure I ever did.
Before it all felt six inches out of reach,
I was too small, my torso too big,
my arms and legs too long,
seasick, dizzy,
looking through fogged glass.

Balance

I thought it might taste sweet,
like the hours spent by the honeysuckle bushes,
dismembering the flowers.

Or, if not sweet,
the sickly wet-dog scent of the dead squirrel
baking on the driveway.
I'm breathing with my mouth open.

But I never expected unbuttered grits, all texture.
I thought when I found it,
stability would taste a lot less
ordinary.

Stability

It's carpenter bees and cutter ants,
looking for four leaf clovers on the soccer field,
sitting outside until the sun goes down,
until midnight in the spring,
while the cicadas scream,
while the mosquitoes are sleeping.
It's catching butterflies in salad bowls,
lightning bugs in jars.
It's watching the clouds roll in,
the downpour,
standing on the front porch,
counting lightning strikes.
It's nostalgia for the future,
making plans and following through,
showing up early with a pack of beer,
chicken sandwiches, casserole.
It's mint tea, crape myrtle rain.
It's skinny dipping,
watching the neighbors close the blinds
and laughing,
knuckle freckles,
an all over tan.

It's remembering drifting out to sea
but not yearning for the weightlessness,
no pounding in my chest,
restful leg syndrome,
freedom.

Not Really the End

I'm not a lily,
or a cypress,
or a sunflower.
A gardener won't come to me with salt.
No roots, I've just got legs,
and after the hurricane,
I still stand,
the torrent, the tsunami,
I still stand,
shoes muddy, socks wet,
uncomfortable
vigorous.